Merry Christmas to our
very special friend.

Love Mary &

Ken

1994

CHILDREN OF WAR,
CHILDREN OF PEACE

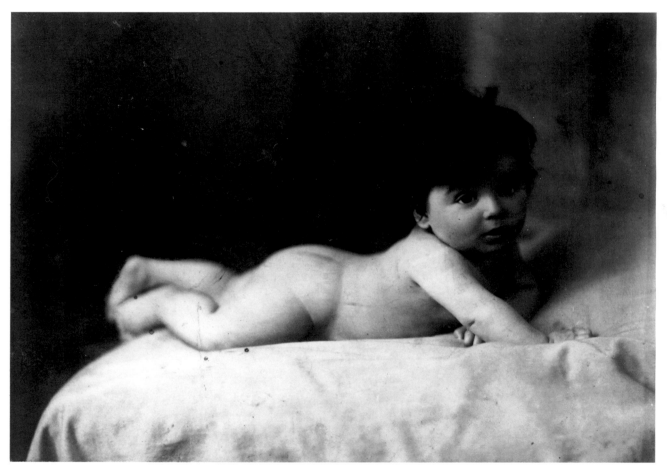

Robert Capa, c. 1914. Anonymous photograph.

CHILDREN OF WAR, CHILDREN OF PEACE

PHOTOGRAPHS BY ROBERT CAPA

EDITED BY CORNELL CAPA & RICHARD WHELAN

A Bulfinch Press Book
Little, Brown and Company
Boston • Toronto • London

First Edition

Library of Congress Cataloging-in-Publication Data
Capa, Robert, 1913 – 1954.
    Children of war, children of peace : photographs by Robert Capa,
    edited by Cornell Capa and Richard Whelan. — 1st ed.
       p.   cm.
    "A Bulfinch Press book."
    Includes bibliographical references.
    ISBN 0-8212-1789-5
    1. Children—Pictorial works.   I. Capa, Cornell.   II. Whelan,
Richard.   III. Title.   IV. Title: Children of war, children of
peace.
HQ781.5.C36   1991
779'.25'092—dc20   90-29879

Bulfinch Press is an imprint and trademark of Little, Brown and Company (Inc.)
Published simultaneously in Canada by Little, Brown & Company (Canada) Limited

PRINTED IN GREAT BRITAIN

This book is dedicated
to my nephew,
Brian Jeffrey Parrella,
born May 31, 1989.
May he live in a world at peace.

R.W.

ACKNOWLEDGMENTS

First and foremost, we want to thank Edie Capa, who has enthusiastically supported, and contributed to, this project from the very beginning. She has suggested images for inclusion, located elusive negatives, and in innumerable other ways provided aid and comfort.

We also extend our heartfelt thanks to Teresa Engle, who has done a superb job of printing the negatives and who has unfailingly met pressured deadlines with good cheer.

In addition, we wish to express our deep gratitude to our agent, Melanie Jackson; to our editor, Ray Roberts; to our copyeditor, Deborah Jacobs; to the Bulfinch production manager, Amanda Freymann; and to our designer, Arnold Skolnick.

This book is published on the occasion of the exhibition *Children of War, Children of Peace: Photographs by Robert Capa* at the International Center of Photography Midtown, in New York, from September through November 1991. The exhibition was made possible by the support of the Professional Photography Division of Eastman Kodak Company and by a generous grant in memory of Jeanne and Charles Korn.

We wish to thank the entire staff of the International Center of Photography and of ICP Midtown for its dedication to and hard work on this project. In particular we want to thank Ann Doherty, Willis Hartshorn, Phyllis Levine, Charles Stainback, and Anna Winand. Finally, we wish to express our special thanks to Richard and Claire Yaffa for their friendship and encouragement.

Cornell Capa & Richard Whelan

CONTENTS

FOREWORD
by Richard Whelan

Before one can come up with an answer, one must realize that there is a question. It has long been recognized that Robert Capa made a number of unforgettable pictures of children. Indeed, it has been acknowledged that some of these pictures are among his most powerfully moving and haunting images. But it simply never occurred to anyone (including, until the spring of 1989, myself) to ask the question, "Do Capa's photographs of children constitute a body of work of sufficient quantity as well as quality to stand on its own?"

Once I had been serendipitously prompted to ask that question, I found myself launched on a treasure hunt that was rewarded at every turn. It seemed as though on every contact sheet and in every folder of vintage prints there was at least one marvelous new discovery—a hitherto-unknown image of classic quality. The question that I then began to ask myself was: "How is it possible that such great images have passed unnoticed until now?" By way of an answer, I was reminded of something that the sculptor Henry Moore once said: "Sometimes for several years running I have been to the same part of the sea-shore—but each year a new shape of pebble has caught my eye, which the year before, though it was there in hundreds, I never saw. Out of the millions of pebbles passed in walking along the shore, I choose out to see with excitement only those which fit in with *my existing form-interest* at the time."*

At his death Robert Capa left behind about 70,000 negatives, spanning his entire career, from 1932 to 1954. Of those 70,000 images perhaps 500 have been published and/or exhibited posthumously. The majority of them have been combat or combat-related pictures from the five wars that Capa covered: the Spanish civil war, the Second Sino-Japanese War, the European theater of World War II, the Israeli War for Independence, and the French Indochina War. That work has been emphasized because Capa is generally categorized as a war photographer.

The truth of the matter, however, is that Robert Capa was always—whether in war or in peace—primarily a photographer of people. It was his lifelong project to document the full range of human experience: to condemn the horrors of war, to celebrate bravery, to revel in the joys of victory and of peace, and to observe the quirks of everyday life. His photographs of children that became well known seemed simply to add up to a minor, though especially fine, chapter in that project. But now that I have gone through all of Capa's work looking specifically for his pictures of children, I am forced to conclude that Capa diligently and consistently sought out children everywhere he went during his career—and that children thus constitute a major, not a minor, theme in his lifework.

We have always known that Robert Capa was tender and loving, but here we see that side of him in its fullest flower. We see his compassion for the children of war, and

*Quoted in Herbert Read, *A Concise History of Modern Sculpture* (New York: Frederick A. Praeger, 1964), p. 178.

his rage at the powers that inflicted suffering upon them. We also see him in poetic and witty moods in peacetime. But he never falls into the most dangerous trap that besets those who photograph children: his pictures are never cute—they always have an edge.

I wrote in the introduction to the collection of Robert Capa's images that I edited with Cornell Capa in 1985 that many of the photographs we had chosen display an unexpectedly strong affinity with the work of André Kertész and of Henri Cartier-Bresson, both of whom were very close friends of Capa's. In common with Kertész, Capa evinced warmth, gentleness, and humor in his photographs; with Cartier-Bresson he shared an epiphanic and yet classical sense of composition as well as a love of both the beauty and the ironies revealed by juxtapositions within the photographic frame. Those aspects of Capa's sensibility are more evident than ever in the present collection, as is an even more unexpected trait: namely, a post-classically sophisticated visual complexity that strikingly anticipates the work that Robert Frank, Lee Friedlander, and Garry Winogrand would make twenty or thirty years later. (See, for instance, the image of the Madrid street performer with a tame bear in 1936 or that of the boys on their bicycles discussing the Tour de France in 1939.) Nor did Capa reject those unconventional pictures as failures to be left unprinted. Vintage prints exist of many such images.

Furthermore, so sure were Capa's eye and reflexes that the editors of this book have found, in almost every case, that cropping the images would have weakened, rather than strengthened, them. Especially when he was using a 35-millimeter camera, Capa composed to the very edges of the frame. Over and over again, as we considered eliminating peripheral details that at first seemed extraneous, we realized that they were actually integral to the picture's balance and immediacy.

Robert Capa cannot be pigeonholed as a war photographer or even as a photojournalist, for, as we see in his photographs of children, he was an artist of great range, mastery, and richness. Not only did he risk his life in the front lines of battle; he also took artistic risks in an effort to increase his ability to express subtle truths and moods. What we see here is a more personal side of Robert Capa than we have ever seen before.

INTRODUCTION
by Cornell Capa

SOON after my brother was killed in Indochina in 1954, John Steinbeck wrote that Bob Capa knew "that you cannot photograph war, because it is largely an emotion. But he did photograph that emotion by shooting beside it. He could show the horror of a whole people in the face of a child."*

Bob Capa, one of the greatest of all war photographers, hated war. He hated it above all because of the terrible suffering that it inflicted upon the innocent—and who could be more innocent than a child? Surely, if anything could induce humankind to renounce war, Bob's photographs of the children of war would do so.

Bob used to say, "In a war you must hate somebody or love somebody." In every war he covered, he was a partisan. Wherever he witnessed fighting, one thing remained constant for him: he was a partisan for the children. It was their anguish that grieved him most. Once—in Barcelona in 1939, as the Spanish civil war was drawing to its tragic close—he photographed a beautiful refugee girl as she waited for transportation from the doomed city; afterward he wrote, with his usual understatement, "It is not always easy to stand aside and be unable to do anything except record the sufferings around one."

Bob despaired for the children of war, but some of them also gave him hope. He repeatedly photographed children playing, or laughing, or at least smiling bravely in the aftermath of battle. In such scenes he clearly saw the indomitable resilience of the human spirit, with its promise of recovery and renewal.

In his postwar photographs of the children of peace, one always senses in the background Bob's memories of war. A child of peace was for him a child who had been spared the horrors of war, a child whose peace had been won at terrible cost, a child whose happiness was therefore all the more precious. If his photographs of the children of war say "This must stop," then his pictures of the children of peace say "This we must never jeopardize again."

My brother was born in Budapest in 1913. At birth he had an extra pinky on one hand. A friendly nanny was quick to interpret that omen to mean that he would be a very lucky and well-beloved person. That prediction turned out to be pretty much on the mark.

Bob (whom we called Bandi in those days) was an engaging child, and everyone—family, friends, and strangers alike—adored him. He was the middle child. László, the eldest, was born in 1911, and I arrived on the scene in 1918. Our parents were kept very busy by the demands of their dressmaking salon, but our mother, Julia, always found time to be loving, possessive, and proud of us. She tried to be fair and impartial with all three of us, but she was especially attentive to Bob. He was a warm and outgoing child; his

*John Steinbeck, "Robert Capa: A Memorial Portfolio," in *Popular Photography*, September 1954.

personality was irresistible, as it would remain throughout the rest of his life. Furthermore, the adventurousness that he began to manifest very early on meant that he needed and desired extra attention.

Bob was only seventeen when he got into serious trouble with the Hungarian government, which was then under the dictatorship of the proto-fascist and anti-Semitic Admiral Miklós Horthy. As a politically precocious (and not very religious) Jewish student, Bob did what rebellious and idealistic students were beginning to do all over Europe: he contacted a Communist party recruiter. During a long walk late at night, the man told Bob that the party was not interested in young bourgeois intellectuals. Conversely, Bob decided that he was not interested in the party. But the damage had been done, for the walk had been observed by the police. Not long after Bob returned home that night, two agents pounded on our apartment door and demanded that Bob get dressed and go with them to police headquarters. Our mother's passionate pleas and reassurances fell on deaf ears, and Bob was taken away.

Fortunately, the wife of the head of the police was a good customer of our parents' salon. Through that connection, our father was able to secure Bob's release the next day—on the condition that the boy leave Hungary at once. It was decided that Bob would go to Berlin, where he could study to become a journalist. And so my seventeen-year-old brother became a political exile. He would never again have a real home.

It is vital to remember that fact as we look at his photographs of the children of war. His experience gave him extraordinary empathy with those children, and that empathy enabled him to make pictures that move us so deeply.

At the end of 1931, his first year in Berlin, Bob learned that because of the effects of the worldwide economic depression, our parents could no longer afford to send him money for his tuition, room, and board. He would have to get a job. But what could an eighteen-year-old without a professional degree do in a country where he couldn't get a work permit and whose language he spoke badly? Become a photographer, of course. Photography is a universal language, a direct means of communication without need of translation.

Bob would become a journalist—a photojournalist. In that case, Berlin was the right place for him to be. The small, fast-lens Leica camera had just been invented, allowing an unemployable foreigner to use his intelligence, eyes, and heart to communicate with the world. The German magazines were using photographs as nobody had before, and the public responded with great enthusiasm. For the first time, leading photojournalists were well paid for their work, and those who got the biggest scoops and who made the most interesting or daring pictures even became celebrities.

Bob's first big break was an assignment to photograph the exiled Russian revolutionary leader Leon Trotsky giving a speech in Copenhagen. The pictures—made surreptitiously with a Leica—were sensational and were given an impressive layout in a major German magazine. But before Bob could enjoy the fruits of his first success, Hitler's sudden rise to power, early in 1933, made a hasty exit from Germany seem advisable. And so Bob made his way to Paris, to develop the art of writing with light in the City of Light.

It was in Paris that Bob began to photograph children in earnest. He was unemployed and wandered through the streets with his camera. Perhaps at first he focused on children simply because they were the only Parisians who would smile at a poor and lonely refugee whose French was far from comme il faut.

Bob soon found a place in the community of talented Eastern European refugees who lived and worked in Montparnasse. He had no money, but he was incredibly charming and resourceful. Gradually the French magazines began to buy his pictures. As the streets filled with the swelling ranks of leftists protesting the rise of fascism and demanding political and economic reforms, Bob photographed the gestures of children mimicking their activist parents. Such images provided a touching, ironic, and sometimes comic perspective on momentous events. Besides, an editor bored with pictures of adult demonstrators might just select an amusing picture of a child for his lead—even if the photographer was an unknown foreigner.

It was in 1936, when the French elected the leftist coalition Popular Front government, that Bob really came into his own. With great passion and commitment, he threw himself into photographing the social and political ferment of the time: the Parisian street theater of constant demonstrations and parades. His pictures captured the tremendous excitement of the period, and soon they began to appear on magazine covers and to be featured in extensive layouts.

The Spanish civil war broke out in July 1936, and Bob—together with his girlfriend Gerda Taro, who was just taking up photography—was among the first photojournalists to make their way to Spain to cover the fighting. He loved Spain, the Spanish people, and, of course, Spanish children. Perhaps the reason he felt so much at home in Spain is that we Hungarians have a great deal in common with the Spaniards; the two nations have a shared heritage of Hapsburgs, Islamic conquerors, Gypsies, and the warm, encompassing mother figure. Above all, however, was the fact that Bob felt that the Spanish fight against fascism was also his own fight.

Committed to the cause, Bob went right up into the front lines in the heat of battle. The pictures he sent back to Paris (where I was developing and printing his negatives in a hotel bathroom) showed war as it had never been shown before—so close up that the magazine reader could almost feel the shock of exploding shells, hear the clatter of machine-gun fire, and experience the soldiers' surges of adrenaline. But when a battle was over, Bob kept on working. During the Spanish civil war, civilians were subjected to aerial bombardment on an unprecedented scale. And so Bob turned his camera toward the elderly, the women, and the children who had been forced from their homes or who had been injured. Of these, he focused especially on the children, whose utter innocence made their victimization all the more tragic and outrageous.

As a bright and adventurous teenager in Budapest, Bob had fallen under the spell of a local artist-poet-editor named Lajos Kassák, who published an avant-garde magazine of art, literature, and politics. Documentary, reform-oriented photographs were published in the magazine, and among the photographers given special attention were the Americans Jacob Riis and Lewis Hine, both of whom are known especially for their powerful pictures of children. (Riis photographed the appalling conditions in which immigrants lived and worked in New York City, while Hine took his pictures of children as part of his lifelong crusade against child labor.) We can only surmise that Bob probably had seen those pictures in Kassák's magazine and that they possibly influenced him to make his own passionate documentation of the plight of children.

That interest of course followed him wherever he went. He journeyed next to China, in 1938, to cover the Chinese resistance to the Japanese invasion—the eastern front of the international antifascist struggle whose western front was in Spain. Bob's pictures of China clearly show that his reaction to that country's fight was: all is the same as in Europe, and yet all is different. The battles, the air raids, the refugees, and the rallies were all very familiar—but the faces, the clothes, the manners, and the language were all different. So were the children, who were more highly disciplined and regimented than their European counterparts. Their formality made their expressive and revealing gestures all the more poignant. And when these children, who at times could seem like human dolls, gave in to their natural high spirits (as they did after a snowstorm in Hankow), Bob's photographs communicate to us an intensified sense of release and exhilaration. It is no wonder that Bob wrote to our mother (was he perhaps half-serious?) saying that he was thinking about adopting a Chinese child to live with us in New York, where what was left of our family (our father and László had both died) settled in the late 1930s.

The child never did materialize, but Bob must certainly have been reminded of his plan when, in 1943, he photographed an American officer in London with some orphaned British girls whom his unit had "adopted." What is so interesting about those pictures is that the kids are responding to the officer in exactly the way I imagine that children all over the world responded to Bob. Once, when Bob was asked for the secret of taking good pictures, he advised, "Like people and let them know it." He certainly loved children and let them know it—and they loved him and trusted him in return.

Throughout World War II Bob was in the forefront of the most intense fighting: in North Africa, in Sicily and on the Italian mainland, on Omaha Beach on D-Day, on the road to Paris, in the Ardennes, and in Germany. Although technically an enemy alien (the United States was at war with Hungary, and Bob was not yet an American citizen), he became a legendary *Life* correspondent accredited by the U.S. Army. Everywhere he photographed not only the frontline action but also the children of war, the children of despair and of hope. Sometimes it seemed as though nothing would ever change: he saw over and over again the same terrible scenes that he had first photographed in Spain. For instance, in 1943, after a week-long battle to drive the Germans out of the Sicilian hilltop town of Troina, he took a picture of a man carrying a girl who is obviously in a state of shock and one of whose legs is heavily bandaged. Six years earlier he had taken a remarkably similar picture in the Spanish hilltop town of Teruel, after a week-long battle to drive out Franco's troops.

At last, however, the tide of battle turned, and it became apparent that the Allies would emerge victorious. Bob delighted in photographing the defeat and the capitulation of the German army. But he took no delight in the sufferings of the German people. His pictures of German families as they faced the hardships of survival amid devastation are sympathetic, not vindictive.

For Bob, one of the most joyous days of the war was that in August 1944 on which the Allies liberated his beloved Paris. During the delirious celebrations he photographed a small child picking his nose while sitting atop a tank turret. I like to think that, in some way not quite translatable into words, that picture says something very profound about Bob's opinion of the entire business of war. He liked the picture well enough to include it in his sardonic book of war memoirs, which he entitled *Slightly Out of Focus.*

After the end of the war, Bob toyed occasionally with the idea of settling down, and even of getting married and having children of his own. But not even Ingrid Bergman, who fell deeply in love with him, could persuade him actually to take such a step. Bob was to remain for the rest of his life a peripatetic photojournalist, with no involvements or possessions that could prevent him from boarding the next plane to wherever a story cropped up. Even in Paris, his home base, he lived in hotel rooms. He never owned a stick of furniture. And although he had one long and serious romance during the last five or six years of his life, he steered well clear of marriage.

His most serious, lifelong romance was a spiritual affair—complete with letters, telegrams, and bunches of florist-delivered red roses—with our mother, Julia. It was an ideal affair, with full hearts and adoration on both sides. Bob kept it that way by making sure that the romance was always conducted across great distances.

During the postwar period he did, however, start a family of sorts. Together with four photographer friends—Henri Cartier-Bresson (a Frenchman), David Seymour (a Polish refugee known to all as "Chim"), George Rodger (an Englishman), and Bill Vandivert (an American)—Bob founded the photo agency Magnum, run as a cooperative by and for the photographers. Once securely established, Magnum began to adopt talented young photographers. It was Bob, as the agency's president, who was especially concerned and involved with these young men and women. He got them assignments, gave them advice, helped them to edit and syndicate their stories, and took them out to dinner and to the races. Even though some of them were barely younger than he was himself, he looked upon them as his children—and loved them and worried about their growth and the flowering of their talents. Magnum became his second family, and his labors of love on its behalf were as close as he ever came to the joys and trials of fatherhood.

Only once in his career did Bob work on a major story specifically about children. In 1954 he was invited by the newly established Mainichi camera magazine to visit Japan to photograph whatever interested him. He chose children as his subject, and for a few weeks he thoroughly enjoyed himself as he focused on young Japanese, in whom he found the same engaging combinations—of discipline and spontaneity, of formality and grace, of precocious maturity and refreshing playfulness—that had so fascinated him in China sixteen years earlier.

While he was in Japan, Bob received a call from *Life* magazine asking him to fill in for a photographer who had to leave Indochina for a month. The Vietminh were on the verge of inflicting a major defeat on the French at Dienbienphu, and Bob decided to accept the assignment. Maintaining the momentum of his work in Japan, he took many wonderful pictures of children in Luang Prabang and Hanoi. Most of these children were still untouched by the war. It wasn't until the last few days of his life that Bob resumed photographing children of war.

On his last day—May 25, 1954—Bob went with a French motor convoy to

Robert Capa arriving in Japan. Tokyo, 1954.

evacuate two small forts in the Red River delta. Along the way he photographed the incongruous juxtaposition of, on the one hand, the massive French armored vehicles and, on the other, the peasants and their children, carrying their produce and driving their ducks to market as they had always done. It was along that road that Bob stepped on a Vietminh land mine and was killed.

A few of Robert Capa's photographs of children have, of course, become classic images over the years. But Richard Whelan realized that children—in peace as well as in war—had been a preoccupation of Bob's everywhere he went throughout his entire career. Richard painstakingly combed through all of Bob's contact sheets and vintage prints and discovered hundreds of marvelous photographs of children, from among which we have chosen the finest to reproduce here. Some of the images are from negatives that have never before been printed, and very few of the photographs in this book have previously been published or shown.

Now, finally, they are revealed, and the pictures have proven to be well worth the wait. Many of them are surely destined to become recognized as classics.

But for myself, the meaning of these pictures is more personal—for here, at last, is Bob Capa's secret family album, his children from everywhere. In these pictures I see the dividends of the love that our parents showered upon him when he was a child and that our mother, Julia, continued to lavish on him throughout his life. Here we can see the love and admiration that he received in such bountiful measure reinvested by him, transferred to children around the world with his own tenderness. In this book are uncovered the secrets of a loving, lonely heart.

Mexico, 1940.

THE PHOTOGRAPHS

Prewar: Hungary, France, & Belgium

Hungary, 1933. A tame wolf.

Paris, 1936. A visit to one of the factories
occupied by sit-in strikers.

Paris, c. 1936.
Jardin du Luxembourg.

Paris, c. 1936.

Paris, c. 1936.

Paris, 1937. Members of a Laurel and Hardy fan club.

Paris, 1936. Watching the Armistice Day parade.

Brussels, 1939. Watching the parade during the state visit of Queen Wilhelmina of the Netherlands.

Paris, 1936. Bastille Day parade during the
heyday of the leftist Popular Front government.

Paris, 1936.
Giving the Popular Front salute at a political rally.

Paris, 1939. Before the race, a Tour de France cyclist with neighborhood children.

Paris, 1939. Discussing the Tour de France.

Pleyben, Brittany, 1939.
Watching the Tour de France.

Pleyben, 1939. Watching the Tour de France.

Arlon, Luxembourg Province, Belgium, 1939.

Spain

Seville, 1935. Feria celebrations.

Madrid, 1936. Street performer with a tame bear.

Seville, 1935. A young participant
in the Holy Week celebrations.

San Sebastian, 1935.

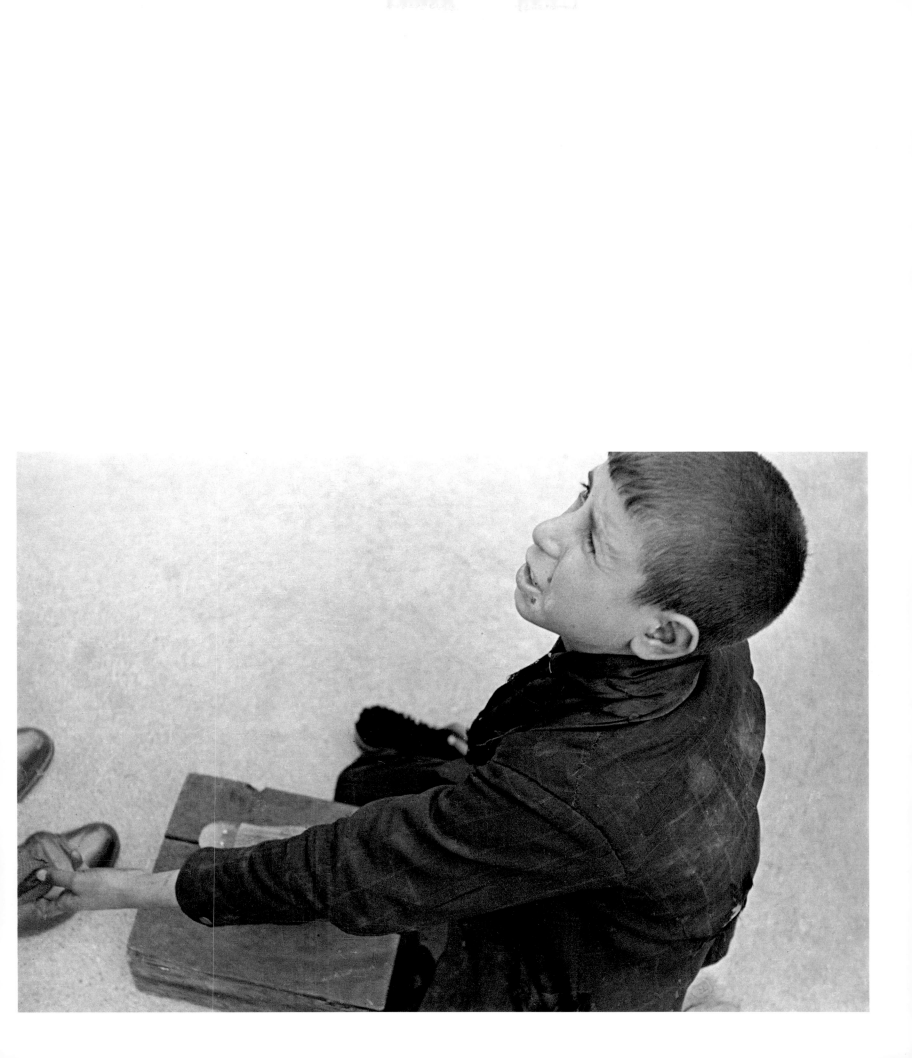

Barcelona, 1936.

Bilbao, 1937. Air-raid alarm.

Barcelona, 1939. A downed enemy plane on display.

Barcelona, 1939. Watching an air battle.

Bilbao, 1937.

Madrid, 1936.

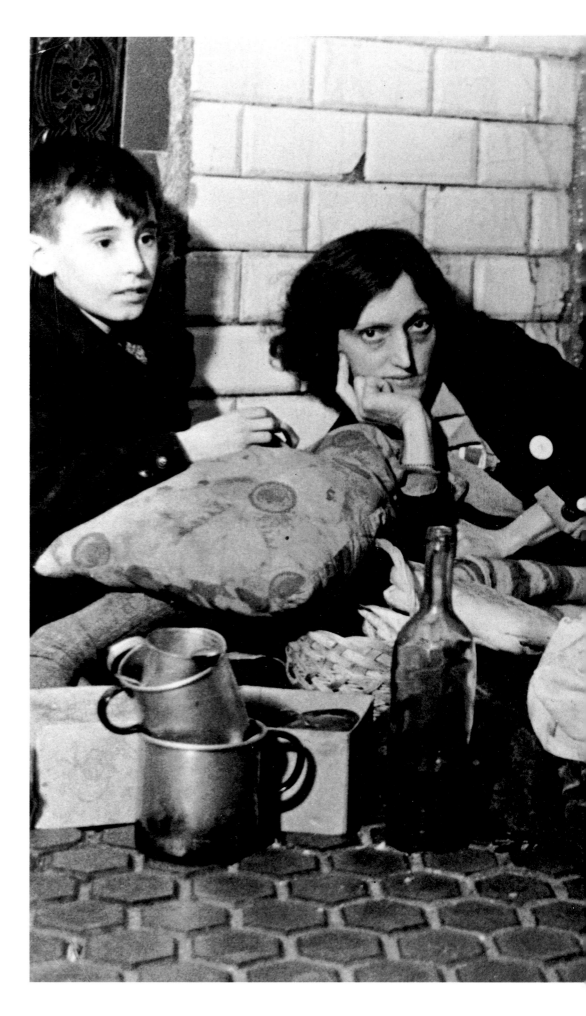

Madrid, 1936.
Living on the platform of a subway station
for refuge from the bombing of the city.

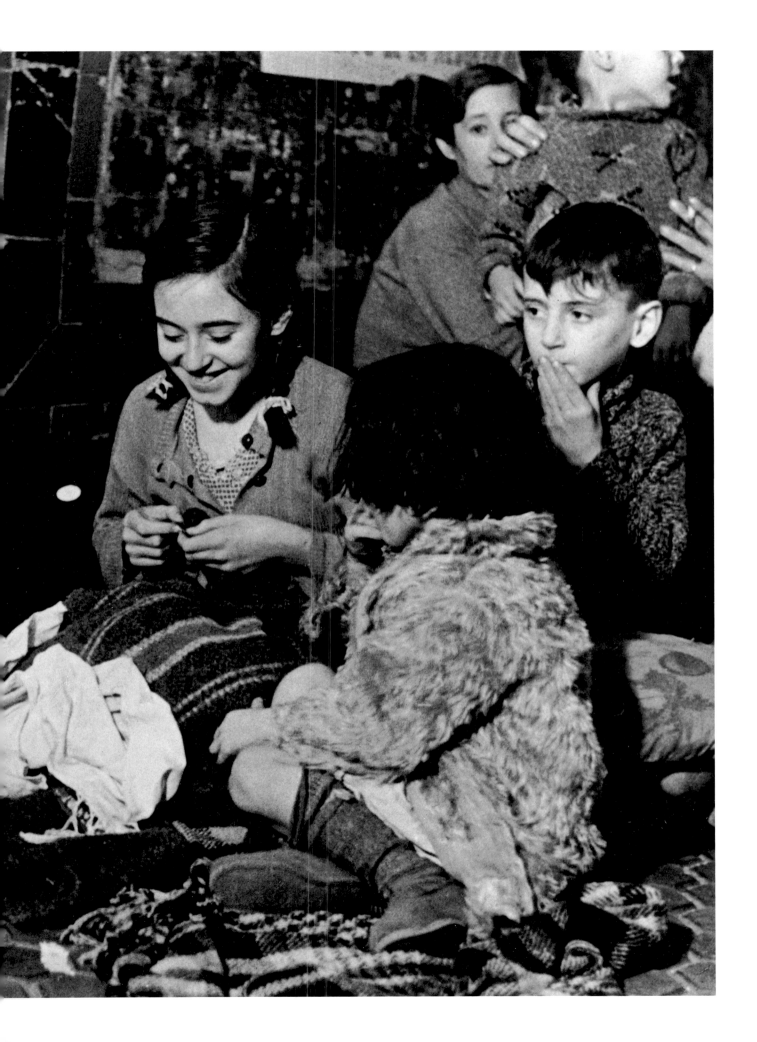

Murcia, 1937. Refugees from Malaga.

Teruel, Aragon Province, 1937.

Barcelona, 1939. Waiting for transport out
of the city as Franco's troops approach.

Barcelona, 1939.
Preparing to abandon the city.

Barcelona, 1939. Preparing to abandon the city.

Near Barcelona, 1939.
Refugees from Tarragona.

Near Barcelona, 1939. Refugees from Tarragona.

On the road from Barcelona to the French border, 1939.

Near Biarritz, France, 1939. Spanish civil war orphans under the care of the Foster Parents' Plan for Spanish Children, largely financed by contributions from Americans.

China

Hankow, 1938.

Hankow, 1938.
Patriotic rally against the
Japanese invasion of China
that had begun the
previous year.

Hankow, 1938.

Hankow, 1938.

Hankow, 1938. Distribution of secondhand clothing.

Near Canton, 1938. At an orphanage.

Xian, 1938.

Hankow, 1938.
Watching a parade.

Hankow, 1938. Watching an air battle.

Hankow, 1938. Watching a parade.

Hankow, 1938. Air-raid alarm.

Near Süchow, 1938. Along the railway carrying troops to the front.

U.S.A.

New York City, 1937. A boxer and his son at Stillman's Gym.

Calumet City, Illinois, 1940.
A bar owner's son having a soft drink.

Ernest Hemingway and his son Gregory,
Sun Valley, Idaho, 1941.

World War II: Britain

London, 1941.

London, 1943. An American officer
with war orphans "adopted" by his unit.

World War II: Italy

Palermo, Sicily, 1943. The arrival of American troops.

Agrigento, Sicily, 1943.

Palermo, 1943.

Troina, Sicily, 1943. American forces had bombed and shelled this hilltop German stronghold for a week. Many Italian civilians had been trapped in the village.

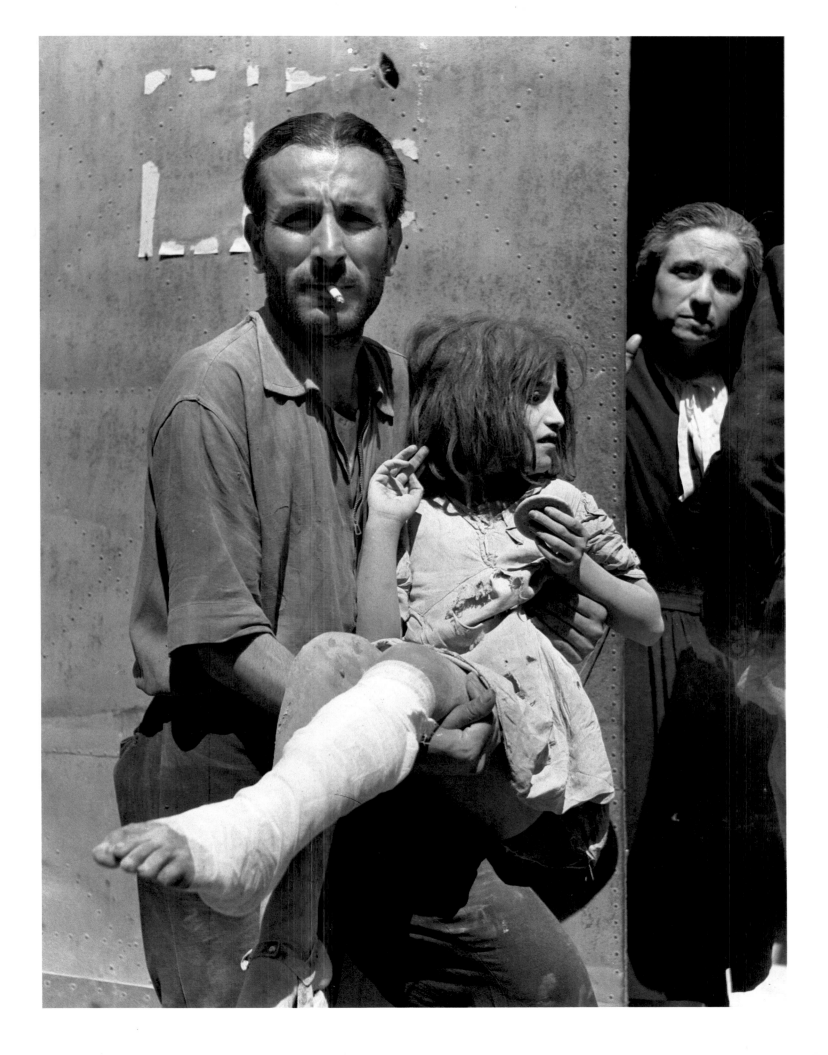

Moscoso Notch (near Cassino), 1944.

Near Cassino, 1944.

World
War II:
France

Paris, 1944.
General Charles de Gaulle
in the parade celebrating the
liberation of the city
from the Germans.

Paris, 1944. Celebrating the liberation.

In the Vercors region, eastern France, 1944.

World War II:
Germany & the Netherlands

Near Wesel, Germany, 1945. After a battle in
which their farmhouse had burned down.

Berlin, 1945.

Nuremberg, 1945.

Berlin, 1945. At the first Rosh Hashanah services
to be held in any of the city's synagogues since 1938,
two Jewish boys who had survived the Holocaust.

Amsterdam, 1945.

Amsterdam, 1945.
A starving Dutch orphan.

The Soviet Union

Moscow, 1947.

Stalingrad, 1947.

Moscow, 1947. Watching the fireworks celebrating the
eight hundredth anniversary of the founding of the city.

Ukraine, 1947. Collective-farm children.

Hungary

Budapest, 1949.

Israel

Haifa, 1949. Immigrants arriving from Europe.

Haifa, 1949. In an "absorption camp" for newly arrived immigrants.

Haifa, 1949–50. Yemeni Jews.

Haifa, 1950. In an absorption camp.

Haifa, 1949–50.

Near Gedera (south of Tel Aviv), 1950. In a then-nameless village for the blind and their families, three men are led toward the community dining hall.

Galilee region, 1949. In an immigrant transit camp.

Jerusalem, 1949. In the Mea Shearim district.

Western Europe

Tromsö, Norway, 1951.

Biarritz, France, 1951. Basque festival.

Françoise Gilot and her son,
Claude Picasso, Vallauris (near Antibes), France, 1949.

Pablo Picasso, Françoise Gilot, and Claude,
Golfe-Juan, France, 1948.

Picasso and Claude, Golfe-Juan, 1948.

Queen Juliana of the Netherlands with her daughter Maryke,
who was born partially blind. Soestdijk Palace,
near Baarn, the Netherlands, 1951.

Japan

Nara, 1954.

Osaka, 1954.

Yaizu, 1954.

Nara, 1954.

Atami, 1954.

Osaka, 1954.

Tokyo, 1954.

Yaizu, 1954.

Tokyo, May Day, 1954.

Tokyo, 1954.

Yaizu, 1954.

Indochina

Luang Prabang, Laos, 1954.

Luang Prabang, 1954.

Hanoi, 1954.

Hanoi, 1954.

On the road from Nam Dinh to Thaibinh, Red River delta,
Vietnam, May 25, 1954. Robert Capa took this picture
a few hours before he was killed by a land mine.

Nam Dinh, May 21, 1954.

Nam Dinh, May 21, 1954.

BIOGRAPHICAL CHRONOLOGY

1913
Born Endre Friedmann, in Budapest, on October 22.

1931
Made contact with a Communist party recruiter, was observed by the secret police, arrested, and released the next day on the condition that he leave Hungary at once. Went to Berlin, where he enrolled that fall at the Deutsche Hochschule für Politik as a student of journalism. At the end of the year learned that his parents, their dressmaking business badly hurt by the Depression, could no longer send him money for tuition, room, and board.

1932
A Hungarian acquaintance helped him to get a job as an errand boy and darkroom assistant at Dephot, an important Berlin photo agency. The director, Simon Guttmann, soon recognized his talent, lent him a camera, and began to send him out to cover minor local events. Received his first big break in December, when Guttmann sent him to Copenhagen to photograph Leon Trotsky giving a speech to Danish students.

1933
Fled Berlin after Hitler assumed dictatorial powers in the wake of the Reichstag fire (February 27). Went to Vienna, then obtained permission to return to Budapest. After a summer living at home and working on local photographic assignments, left in September for Paris, where he hoped to find success as a photojournalist. Instead, at first, he found hunger, which was mitigated only by the camaraderie of the artistic community of Hungarian and German refugees in Montparnasse.

1934
Met Gerda Taro, a young German who became his lover and, in effect, his business manager. Began to teach her the basics of photography.

1935
Went to Spain to work on several photojournalistic assignments arranged for him by Simon Guttmann.

1936
Invented a glamorous and successful American photographer named Robert Capa; made the photographs that Gerda Taro sold to impressed editors as Capa's. The ruse was soon discovered, and he changed his own name to Robert Capa. Covered the tumultuous events in Paris surrounding the election of the leftist coalition Popular Front government, headed by socialist Léon Blum. The Spanish civil war broke out in July. Went to Spain with Gerda Taro in August to cover the Republican government's resistance to Franco's fascist rebels. Made a second trip to Spain in November to photograph the defense of Madrid.

1937

Visited various fronts in Spain, alone and with Gerda Taro, who was herself becoming an independent photojournalist. In July, while he was taking care of business in Paris, Taro covered the fighting at Brunete, west of Madrid. During a confused retreat she was crushed to death by a Loyalist tank. Capa, who had hoped to marry her, never fully recovered from his grief. In September, made his first trip to the United States, to visit his mother and brother Cornell in New York and to negotiate a contract with *Life* magazine.

1938

Spent six months in China with filmmaker Joris Ivens documenting the Chinese resistance to the Japanese invaders.

1939

Covered the fall of Barcelona. After the end of the Spanish civil war, in March, photographed the defeated and exiled Republican soldiers in internment camps in France. Worked on various stories in France, including an extensive one about the Tour de France. After the outbreak of World War II, in September, sailed for New York, where he began to work on miscellaneous stories for *Life*.

1940

Spent several months in Mexico, covering the Mexican presidential campaigns and elections for *Life*.

1941

Spent the summer in London documenting the city's recovery from the blitz. In October, went to Sun Valley, Idaho, to visit his friend Ernest Hemingway, whom he had first met in Spain.

1942

Crossed the Atlantic in a convoy carrying American planes to England. Worked on numerous stories about the Allied war effort in Britain.

1943

From March to May, covered the Allied victories in North Africa. During July and August, photographed the Allied conquest of Sicily. For the rest of the year, documented the fighting in mainland Italy, including the liberation of Naples.

1944

In January, participated in the Allied landing at Anzio, south of Rome. On D-Day (June 6) landed with the first wave of American troops on Omaha Beach, Normandy. Accompanied American and French troops throughout the campaign that culminated in the liberation of Paris (August 25). In December, covered the Battle of the Bulge in the Ardennes.

1945

Parachuted with American troops into Germany and chronicled the Allied capture of Leipzig, Nuremberg, and Berlin. Met Ingrid Bergman in Paris in June and began a two-year affair with her.

1946

Became an American citizen. Spent several months in Hollywood, writing his war memoirs (on which he intended to base a screenplay) and training to become a producer-director. Finally, decided that he did not like the movie business and left Hollywood. Late in the year, spent two months in Turkey working on a documentary film.

1947

Together with friends Henri Cartier-Bresson, David Seymour ("Chim"), George Rodger, and William Vandivert, founded Magnum, a cooperative photo agency. Spent a month traveling in the Soviet Union with his friend John Steinbeck. Also visited Czechoslovakia and Budapest.

1948-50

Made three trips to Israel. On the first, photographed the declaration of Israel's independence and covered the fighting that followed. On the two subsequent trips, concentrated on the plight of refugees arriving in the country.

1949

Visited Hungary, Poland, and Czechoslovakia with Theodore H. White.

1950-53

Lived in Paris and served as president of Magnum, devoting much time to the agency's business and to the recruitment and promotion of young photographers. Close friends included director John Huston, novelist Irwin Shaw, and columnist Art Buchwald. Enjoyed a glamorous life of afternoons at the Parisian racetracks, evenings at nightclubs with beautiful women, and skiing vacations in Switzerland. Not only made photographs but also wrote the text for amusing articles about his travels to such places as Norway, Deauville and Biarritz (France), and Alpine ski resorts, as well as about his weekend visit with the Dutch royal family. Because of false accusations that he had been a Communist, the U.S. government suspended his passport for several months in 1953, during which time he was unable to travel for his work. Also suffered that year from severe back pain, for which he had to be hospitalized.

1954

In April, spent several weeks in Japan as the guest of the Mainichi press, which was launching a new camera magazine. Focused particularly on Japanese children. At the end of April, while still in Japan,

received a request from *Life* to fill in for its
photographer in Indochina, who had to return to the
United States for a month. Accepted the assignment
and arrived in Hanoi early in May. Then went to
Luang Prabang, Laos, to photograph the wounded
French soldiers captured at Dienbienphu, whom the
Vietminh had agreed to release. Back in Hanoi, spent
several days photographing the life of the city. On
May 25 accompanied a French convoy whose mission
was to evacuate two indefensible outposts in the Red
River delta, where Vietminh activity was increasing.
While the convoy was halted at one point, he went
with a detachment of soldiers out into a field beside
the road. He stepped on a land mine and was killed.

1955
Life and the Overseas Press Club established the
annual Robert Capa Award "for superlative
photography requiring exceptional courage and
enterprise abroad."

1974
Spurred in part by his determination to keep alive
the work of Robert Capa and other photojournalists,
Robert's brother and fellow photojournalist Cornell
Capa founded the International Center of Photog-
raphy in New York City.

BIBLIOGRAPHY

Books by Robert Capa

Death in the Making. Photographs by Robert Capa and Gerda Taro. Captions by Robert Capa, translated by Jay Allen. Preface by Jay Allen. Layout by André Kertész. New York: Covici, Friede, 1938.

The Battle of Waterloo Road. Text by Diana Forbes-Robertson. Photographs by Robert Capa. New York: Random House, 1941.

Invasion! Text by Charles C. Wertenbaker. Photographs by Robert Capa. New York: Appleton, Century, 1944.

Slightly Out of Focus. Text and photographs by Robert Capa. New York: Henry Holt, 1947.

A Russian Journal. Text by John Steinbeck. Photographs by Robert Capa. New York: Viking, 1948.

Report on Israel. Text by Irwin Shaw. Photographs by Robert Capa. New York: Simon and Schuster, 1950.

Books About Robert Capa

Images of War. Photographs by Robert Capa, with text from his own writings. New York: Grossman, 1964.

Robert Capa. Edited by Anna Farova. New York: Grossman, 1969.

Robert Capa. Edited by Cornell Capa and Bhupendra Karia. (ICP Library of Photographers.) New York: Grossman, 1974.

Robert Capa. Edited by Romeo Martinez. Milan: Mondadori, 1979.

Robert Capa. [Catalogue of an exhibition curated by Cornell Capa.] Tokyo: Pacific Press Service, 1980.

Robert Capa. [Catalogue of an exhibition curated by Cornell Capa, Hiroji Kubota, and Richard Whelan.] Tokyo: Pacific Press Service, 1984.

Robert Capa: A Biography, by Richard Whelan. New York: Alfred A. Knopf, 1985.

Robert Capa: Photographs. Edited by Cornell Capa and Richard Whelan. New York: Alfred A. Knopf, 1985.

Robert Capa. Introduction by Jean Lacouture. (Collection Photo Poche.) Paris: Centre National de la Photographie, 1988.

Designer
Arnold Skolnick

Typographer
Ultracomp Inc., New York

Printer
Balding & Mansell, Wisbech, Cambs., England